Text Cop

ALL RIGHTS RESERVED. This book contains material protected under international and federal copyright laws and treaties. Any unauthorized reprint or use of this material is prohibited. No part of this book may be reproduced or transmitted in any form or by any means, electronic or mechanical, including photocopying, recording, or by any information storage and retrieval system without express written permission from the author.

Table of Contents

Chapter 1: Libra Personality Profile 4

Chapter 2: Libra Love and Friendship 22

Chapter 3: Libra Compatibility With Other Sun Signs 25

    Libra + Aries 26

    Libra + Taurus 28

    Libra + Gemini 30

    Libra + Cancer 33

    Libra + Leo 35

    Libra + Virgo 38

    Libra + Libra 41

    Libra + Scorpio 43

    Libra + Sagittarius 45

    Libra + Capricorn 47

    Libra + Aquarius 50

    Libra + Pisces 52

Chapter 4: Libra Marriage 54

    Libra Men: Marriage Rates 55

    Libra Women: Marriage Rates 56

    Some Notes on Marriage Rates 57

Divorce 59

The Best Romantic Match for Libra 61

Chapter 5: Why Some Signs Are More Compatible With Libra Than Others 63

Chapter 6: Libra Children 71

Chapter 7: Libra Parents 73

Chapter 8: Libra Health and Safety 75

Chapter 9: Libra Attitudes, Preferences, and Lifestyles ... 77

Chapter 10: Libra Interests, Hobbies, and Leisure Activities 83

Chapter 11: Libras Behaving Badly 88

Chapter 12: Libra Stuff 90

Chapter 13: Libra Studies 92

Chapter 14: Libra Careers 94

Appendix 1: Libra Associations 98

Appendix 2: Famous Libras 100

Appendix 3: Moon Signs, Ascendants (Rising Signs), and Other Planets 106

References 118

Image Credits 119

Chapter 1: Libra Personality Profile

Ruling Planet: Venus

Element: Air

Symbol: The scales

Quality: Cardinal

Libra Traits: charismatic, conflict-avoidant, diplomatic, fair-minded, fickle, flirtatious, frivolous, graceful, idealistic, indecisive, intellectual, laid back, logical, open-minded, outgoing, reasonable, relationship-oriented, romantic, tolerant

Charismatic

Most Libras have no problem making friends because they have good social skills and tend to be easygoing and friendly. They are naturally charming and flirtatious, and their charisma and tendency to flatter others ensure that many people seek out their company, so they usually have plenty of companions and romantic prospects.

The natural charisma Libras possess gives them the power to influence those around them. Most will use this power for good reasons, such as preventing or ending conflicts. However, many also use their charm to secure favors, and a small minority abuse their charismatic powers to manipulate others in more serious ways. Despite this risk, most Libras use their ability to win friends and influence people primarily to maintain harmonious relations in their social and work lives.

Some Libras draw upon their natural charisma in their careers, gravitating toward fields where they can work with the public and have opportunities to assist and influence clients or customers. Libra charisma is also an asset for those who seek to change the world by joining or even leading political and social movements or participating in volunteer organizations.

Conflict-avoidant

Unless other elements in their natal zodiacs* create more forceful personalities, Libras tend to be conflict-avoidant (to a near-pathological level in some cases). Typical Libras avoid conflict at all costs, and would rather give in than have an unnecessary argument (or in some cases, a necessary one). Arguments make Libras miserable. They crave peace, and much of their lives are spent in the pursuit of harmony and idealized relationships.

Libras have a strong need to be liked by others and they will often suppress or hide their own feelings and opinions to achieve this. They are very concerned with what others think of them, so they nearly always put their best face forward and don't show extremes of emotion, make scenes in public, or criticize others. In some cases, Libra conflict avoidance may even extend to deception because they are so desperate to keep the peace.

---

* The natal zodiac refers to the positions of the planets in the sky at the time of birth. Important influences in the natal zodiac include the sun sign (the one most people know), the moon sign, and the rising sign (also known as the ascendant). Other elements in the natal zodiac can influence how the sun sign is expressed. For example, a Libra with Aries or Leo rising will be more assertive than a typical Libra.

Libras are often perceived as very easygoing because they are quick to compromise, but in many cases, they give in not because they don't care about an issue, but because they don't want to upset anyone. As a result, they may not get their own needs met, and if a relationship fails to meet their requirements, rather than demanding what they want and potentially triggering conflict, they are inclined to slip away in search of a partner or friend who meets their needs without having to ask (this search often ends in disappointment, as most people cannot intuit the needs of their friends or partners, so they require more direct requests to understand what others want).

Diplomatic

Libras are the diplomats of the zodiac. They are willing to conceal their own desires and opinions to preserve good relations with others, and are often called upon to intervene in other people's conflicts because they have a knack for encouraging peaceful compromises.

Libras are among the more tactful astrological signs unless other elements in their natal zodiacs (for example, Aries or Sagittarius rising) incline them to be more blunt and abrasive. They are typically courteous and careful to avoid offending others or causing hurt feelings. In arguments, they don't typically resort to low blows or use other people's vulnerabilities against them.

Fair-minded

Libra is the sign of balance, and the ability to see all sides of an issue that underlies Libran diplomacy skills also makes the typical Libra very fair-minded. Libras examine issues from various perspectives, and they will usually change their minds if new evidence is presented rather than stubbornly clinging to beliefs that are not backed up by facts or that unfairly disadvantage other people.

Although they tend to avoid conflict in their personal lives, many Libras are champions of the underdog and will stick up for others who are being treated unfairly in almost any situation. They won't hesitate to speak up when they see an injustice, even if they don't particularly like the victim. Although they shrink away from conflict in their personal lives, Libras will courageously defend those who are being unfairly maligned or otherwise mistreated.

Fickle

The mental flexibility that enables Libras to see issues from various sides and adapt their beliefs in response to new information can make them appear fickle. Fickle people are those whose affections, loyalties, beliefs, or interests change suddenly or frequently.

Libras are quick to abandon beliefs if they encounter good evidence against them, and they are also inclined to leave people who do not meet their needs and those who like to fight. They tend to make these changes without warning to avoid prolonged arguments, and those who are left behind may interpret this behavior as a lack of loyalty or an inability to care about others.

Libras may appear to slip easily in and out of relationships, friendships, jobs, or groups without giving the matter much thought, which can make them appear cold and unfeeling. However, in reality, they have usually spent much time agonizing over these decisions, but once their minds are made up, they like to exit quietly, without having to endure distressing emotional drama or strife.

Flirtatious

Libras are naturally flirtatious. This doesn't mean they are more likely to cheat on their partners than those of other signs; they just like engaging in playful interactions with others.

Libras enjoy flattering others and making them feel good about themselves, so flirtations may be partly motivated by a desire to please that arises from altruistic motivations. However, Libras also have a desperate need to be liked by everyone, so they often use flirtation as a way of making themselves more likable and popular.

Frivolous

Libra is often characterized as somewhat frivolous by traditional astrologers, but this may be an illusion caused by the sign's carefree appearance. Because Libras don't like to upset others, they tend to act as though they haven't got a care in the world, even when they are suffering significant distress. This can make them appear as though their lives are very light and easy, that nothing really gets to them and they don't experience any strong feelings.

Libras may also appear frivolous due to their love of luxury and the strong desire to be liked that drives some Libras to become obsessive about their appearance. In such cases, vanity motivates them to spend large amounts of money on items to improve their looks or objects that are only for show.

Libras usually keep their bodies and their clothing, other possessions, and homes very neat, and although they have a lazy streak, this almost never extends to personal grooming (it is very uncommon to find a Libra with unbrushed hair or wearing sloppy or dirty clothing). Libras tend to follow fashion trends, but only the ones that are elegant, classy, and have some staying power.

The Libra tendency toward vanity that arises from a desperate need to be liked by everyone makes this sign highly susceptible to flattery. Libras should be aware of this vulnerability because it can be exploited by unscrupulous individuals who want to take advantage of them.

Graceful

Libras are known for their gracefulness. This may manifest as elegance in dress and manner, or an athletic grace that inclines them toward particular sports.

Many Libras do well at pursuits that require physical grace or balance, such as skating, dancing, yoga, Thai chi, or martial arts. However, their good social skills and cooperative abilities also suit them to team sports.

Idealistic

Libras tend to be idealistic, which inclines them toward optimism. They believe that all situations can be improved, even in the face of daunting odds, and their faith in the possibility of creating a better future draws many Libras into political or social movements.

While Libra idealism is largely a positive force, it can create problems because Libras are inclined to leave imperfect romantic relationships, friendships, jobs, or places in search of idealized, unattainably perfect situations. As a result, they may drift from one partner, group of friends, career, or residence to the next, always searching for an impossible ideal. One of the most significant challenges for this sign is to develop more realistic expectations regarding people and environments.

Indecisive

The downside of the ability to entertain multiple perspectives is that Libras tend to be very indecisive (unless their ascendants fall in more single-minded signs such as Aries, Taurus, Leo, Scorpio, or Capricorn). Libras can become so paralyzed by indecision that they are unable to take any course of action, which can make them appear wishy-washy or noncommittal to others.

Libras can spend hours, days, weeks, or even years agonizing over a decision, weighing all the options, examining all the alternatives in depth, and becoming distressed about what would be lost by choosing one option over another or the possibility of making an incorrect choice. As a result, they are at risk for staying in bad situations or missing out on opportunities. A major challenge for this sign is learning how to commit quickly to a course of action when the situation requires it.

Intellectual

Libras need a lot of intellectual stimulation, so most do plenty of reading and spend lots of time discussing issues with others. Their combination of rationality and idealism often manifests as an interest in politics or social issues.

Libras tend to process things logically rather than emotionally unless their ascendants are in water signs (Cancer, Scorpio, or Pisces). This emotional detachment enables them to make calm, unbiased assessments of situations and people. While this is largely a positive trait, it can distress more emotional types who prefer intuitive responses and emotionally expressive interactions.

Laid Back

Libras have a reputation for being laid back, as though nothing bothers them. However, this is to some degree an illusion caused by the Libra tendency to let things go or compromise to avoid fighting. Libras may seem not to care about much because they are so willing to concede a point or go along with what others want, but this is attributable to the Libra desire to keep the peace rather than an uncaring attitude.

Libras are not prone to emotional displays, and they are more likely to speak calmly about issues and think about them rationally rather than giving in to intense feelings, which can make them appear heartless to more sensitive types. They tend to be somewhat detached from their feelings, avoiding emotional pain by defaulting to thinking about things rather than giving free reign to their emotional responses.

Logical

Libras tend to be logical rather than intuitive. Because they have trouble making decisions, they like to examine different courses of action in an objective manner, considering all possible outcomes associated with a particular course of action rather than making decisions based on gut feelings.

Their logical natures ensure that Libras are very reasonable and rational in most cases. They are not inclined to act on blind faith or accept arguments that are not backed by evidence, which can aggravate those who try to persuade them with displays of emotion.

Open-minded

Libras are among the more open-minded signs of the zodiac. They are willing to consider other perspectives and ideas rather than dismissing anything that doesn't accord with their own beliefs and prejudices, and to change their beliefs if new, compelling evidence is presented rather than clinging stubbornly to ideas that are not supported by facts.

Libras will give anyone a fair hearing. They are not inclined to ignore someone for being unpopular or expressing views that are at odds with the majority opinion. When presented with a new perspective, they look at the evidence for both sides rather than rejecting a new idea because they have been brought up to believe something else, or their social groups hold contrary opinions.

Outgoing

Libras are extroverted unless their rising signs incline them to be more solitary (a Libra with Pisces, Cancer, Virgo, Scorpio, or Capricorn rising would need more alone time than a typical Libra).

Libras tend to be socially adept, able to make a good first impression and move smoothly through different types of social situations. They seek companions who can provide intellectual stimulation by discussing issues thoughtfully and in depth (those who shut down discussions by simply telling others they're wrong while presenting no evidence or valid arguments are particularly repellant to Libras). Libras also need to be seen and admired, and to flirt, even if they have no interest in taking things further, which motivates them to go out and interact on a regular basis.

Reasonable

Libras are among the more reasonable signs of the zodiac. Sensible, fair, and moderate in their judgments (unless their ascendants are in signs more prone to extremes, such as Scorpio), Libras seek consensus and compromise, and they don't expect to get their way on every issue. They understand that other people's perspectives and needs are as important and valid as their own, and they're not inclined to demand unreasonable concessions or take more than their fair share of anything.

Because they are reasonable by nature, Libras don't usually rush to judgement. If it seems as though another person has done something wrong, they prefer to wait and gather evidence rather than jumping to conclusions and ending romantic relationships or friendships in a fit of fury.

Relationship-oriented

The sign of Libra is associated with partnerships, and typical Libras have a strong need to be in a relationship at all times. As a result, they may rush into new relationships on the rebound from others, which is often a terrible mistake. Many Libras find it so psychologically difficult to be on their own that they may settle for bad relationships (at least until they can find something better) rather than staying single. However, some can at least partially meet their need for a soul mate platonically with one or more very close friendships, which gives them time to be choosier about their romantic prospects.

Because Libras prefer to be with others (both romantically and platonically) rather than on their own, those with an entrepreneurial streak will usually do better working with a business partner. Libras also tend to work well with groups and are inclined to befriend coworkers (unless they are working in very socially toxic environments).

Typical Libras maintain a wide circle of friends and acquaintances. They are good at keeping up with people, even when relationships are maintained over a distance, and they often do the work of planning social events to ensure that everyone gets together regularly.

Romantic

Most Libras have a strong romantic streak that overwhelms their intellect in relationships. Sometimes they fall in love more with the idea of being in love than with their actual partners, and they have a tendency to put their partners up on pedestals from which they inevitably fall. As a result, Libras are frequently disillusioned. Still, they keep trying because Libra is a sign that needs to be in a partnership to feel complete, and Libras are willing to put up with a lot in order to achieve this.

If their relationships deteriorate to the point where fights occur regularly, Libras will quietly slide out of them, in some cases finding another partner before completely disengaging from the first one. This tendency has earned the sign a reputation for being fickle, but it actually results from an intense dislike of conflict combined with the need to be in a partnership at all times.

The Libra romantic streak can spill over into their views of and expectations for the world. They may have overly idealistic notions about human relationships in general, or propose solutions to the world's problems that do not take the more negative aspects of human nature into account.

Tolerant

Libra is among the more tolerant signs of the zodiac. Typical Libras are less likely to be bigots because bigoted views are irrational and lead to the sort of discord Libras hate. They prefer to live and let live rather than forcing others to conform to their own lifestyle preferences or beliefs. Because they are less prejudiced than most, Libras often stick up for members of groups other than their own.

Libras are also very tolerant in their interpersonal relationships. They let others have their way on a variety of issues, ranging from household décor to social activities. They are very tolerant of the quirks and idiosyncrasies of others (provided those quirks don't include a terrible temper or a penchant for cruelty).

Because they are so tolerant by nature, typical Libras make pleasant companions, unless their rising signs incline them to be more aggressive and temperamental (Aries rising, for example).

The Atypical Libra

The sun sign isn't the only element that influences personality. Aspects and planetary placements, particularly the moon sign and rising sign (ascendant), are also important. For example, a Libra with Aries rising will be far more assertive, decisive, and combative than a typical Libra, and with Cancer rising, a Libra will be more sensitive and intuitive.

There are many websites that offer free chart calculation to determine other planetary placements and aspects. Learning about these other planetary placements and aspects is recommended, as it provides a more comprehensive personality profile.

See Appendix 3 for information about other astrological influences on personality and how to find your rising sign, moon sign, and other planetary placements and aspects.

Chapter 2: Libra Love and Friendship

Peaceful and reasonable by nature, the typical Libra is pleasant, charming company for friends and lovers. However, Libras do have a tendency to be indecisive and conflict-avoidant, which can irritate more assertive types. Perhaps to compensate for their difficulty in making decisions, Libras are often drawn to decisive, strong-willed, and even stubborn individuals.

Relationship Needs

Preserving harmonious relations with friends and lovers at all times is extremely important to Libras. They prefer not to argue and usually won't rise to any sort of bait, which can make relationships very smooth. However, some of the more forthright zodiacal types may perceive Libras as deceptive because they tend to hide their feelings (or in some cases, lie outright) to preserve the peace.

Given their tendency to avoid making waves, Libras may be easy to live with but hard to know. However, their diplomacy also reduces the likelihood of escalating conflicts in friendships or romantic relationships. Typical Libras are not inclined to make emotional scenes or pick fights, and they tend to handle disagreement in a classy and restrained manner.

Because they tend to be gracious, charming, and socially adept, Libras usually have many friends, and they are compelled to go out and interact frequently, as well as to flirt with and charm others. However, they also have a powerful need for a permanent partner, without which they feel incomplete.

Libras are inclined to give others a fair hearing, listening with an open mind to the other person's side of an argument before making up their minds, and they reason things through rather than responding with knee-jerk emotional reactions. They do best with partners who take the same open-minded, calm approach, and have difficulty with those who become emotional during arguments.

Ideal partners and friends for Libra are extroverted, laid back, open-minded, patient, and non-combative. Those who are too pushy or domineering cause Libras to retreat and evade.

Relationship Challenges

Libras like to explore an issue from all angles, so friends and lovers who pressure them for quick decisions or demand that they automatically side with one person over another can cause great anxiety. A particularly traumatic situation for a Libra is one in which two friends have a falling out with the Libra caught in the middle.

Some Libras take conflict avoidance to nearly pathological levels, making themselves scarce whenever a partner or friend wants to discuss any emotionally charged issue. When Libras enter into long-term relationships, they must force themselves to express their feelings, even those that might cause friction, or they may become resentful toward their partners for not understanding them.

Chapter 3: Libra Compatibility With Other Sun Signs

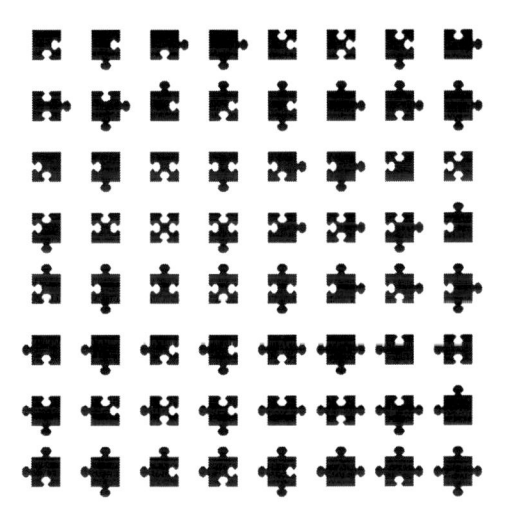

Note: There is more to astrological compatibility than sun signs alone. Other elements in a person's natal zodiac also play a role. Ascendants (rising signs), moon signs, and other planetary placements and aspects also shape personality and affect compatibility. For example, a Capricorn with Leo rising will be more extroverted than a typical Capricorn, and an Aries with Libra rising or the moon in Aquarius will be more compatible with Libra than a typical Aries. For more information on other natal zodiac elements, see Appendix 3.

Libra + Aries

Aries and Libra are often drawn together by mutual attraction, but Libra's desire to avoid conflict is at odds with Aries directness and combativeness. As a result, Aries confronts and provokes while Libra avoids and escapes, leading to a communication breakdown.

The primary source of conflict between these two signs is that Libra craves peace and harmony while Aries wants passion and excitement. Libra seeks smooth social interactions, while Aries needs to stir things up to keep them interesting. Libra tends to be tolerant, easy going, and mellow (to the point of laziness in some cases), whereas Aries is action-oriented, decisive, and anything but calm. Libra is open-minded and can see both sides of an issue, while Aries takes sides and fiercely defends a particular point of view.

Libra's tendency to agonize over decisions will be particularly irritating for Aries, who makes decisions quickly and easily. This conflict of styles can lead to a mutual lack of respect because Aries values strength, dominance, and assertiveness, while Libra appreciates rationality and fair-mindedness. In a worst-case scenario, Aries will view Libra as weak and wishy-washy and Libra will find Aries domineering, abrasive, and egotistical. On the other hand, in some cases these two can balance one another out nicely.

In a best-case scenario, laid-back Libra will have a beneficial calming effect on Aries, while Aries makes decisions for the couple, absolving Libra of this unpleasant responsibility. Ideally, Aries will learn how to adopt a calmer, more thoughtful approach to life from Libra, and Libra will grow more assertive as a result of spending time with Aries, so that both can develop more well-balanced temperaments.

Despite their many differences, there is some common ground to unite these two signs. Aries and Libra both tend to be extroverted, so they are likely to enjoy an active social life together. Also, Aries is typically physical and active, and Libra graceful and athletic, so sports and other physical pursuits may form the basis of shared interests for this pair.

Libra + Taurus

Although conventional astrological wisdom suggests that Taurus and Libra are not compatible, this pairing does have a number of things going for it. Libra wants to maintain peace and harmony and Taurus is laid back, tolerant, and slow to anger, so fights are less likely with this combination than with many other sun-sign pairs (unless Libra's flirtatiousness triggers the infamous Taurean jealousy).

Taurus and Libra share a love of luxury and decadence, and may encourage one another to become lazy. With their strong aesthetic senses, they can create a beautiful home together and because both like to acquire material things, they will fill it with attractive objects if they have the money to do so. Both enjoy entertaining, so their home will be a center of enjoyable social activity. In romance, this is a sensual combination with plenty of chemistry.

Despite its many positive elements, the Taurus-Libra match can be challenging because these two individuals have very different ways of interacting with the world. Taurus tends to be practical, whereas Libras are not inclined to deny themselves anything, which can lead to conflicts over finances. In addition, the typical Taurus is a homebody and prefers to stick with long-term friends rather than venturing out in search of new companions, whereas Libra wants to get out and mingle. If Taurus insists on too may cozy evenings at home in front of the fire or with the same set of friends, Libra may wander off in search of a more extroverted partner (this pairing works best if the Libra has a more introverted ascendant or the Taurus has a more gregarious rising sign).

Another problem with this pairing is that Libra tends to be indecisive and somewhat emotionally detached, placing more emphasis on thoughts than feelings. As a result, Taurus might find Libra emotionally cold. Also, Tauruses are slow boilers, but when their tempers flare, they can be terrifying, and faced with an angry partner, conflict-avoidant Libra will seek the quickest available escape route. This pair has a better chance of success if other elements in their natal zodiacs are more compatible.

Libra + Gemini

This is usually a great combination unless other elements in the two natal zodiacs are highly incompatible. Both signs are sociable, intellectually focused, open-minded, and friendly. They enjoy many of the same things and even when their interests diverge, they allow one another the freedom to pursue activities and friendships outside their primary relationship without assuming that encounters with others will lead to cheating (neither sign is inclined to be jealous). These two can enjoy themselves in social situations, even engaging in their penchant for flirtation without having to worry about facing a partner's wrath (unless one member of the pair has a more possessive rising sign such as Taurus, Cancer, Leo, or Scorpio).

Although they have much in common, there are some important differences between Libra and Gemini. Both like to socialize and flirt, but Libra typically prefers to do so in comfortable, luxurious surroundings, whereas Gemini doesn't care as long as there are new and interesting people to play with. Libra tends to be decadent or even lazy, whereas Gemini is a restless bundle of energy. However, these are not the sort of differences that trigger serious conflict.

Because Libras love peace and Geminis would rather analyze a situation than fight about it, strife is less likely with this pairing than with many other sun-sign combinations. Neither sign is inclined to dominate, so power struggles are also unlikely. Both individuals are tolerant, flexible, open-minded, and willing to compromise, which helps to keep things running smoothly. However, the flipside of this is that both signs can see all sides of an issue, so neither is good at making decisions. With no strong, decisive individual in the partnership, many things may be left undone or unaddressed. When Gemini and Libra pair up, there tends to be a lot of talk but little action, which can be problematic when making major life decisions or trying to run a business.

The other potential problem with this duo is that neither is particularly good with money unless their ascendants fall in more pragmatic signs such as Taurus, Virgo, Scorpio, or Capricorn. Libras don't deny themselves any of life's luxuries and Geminis live in the moment, not thinking about the future consequences of present actions. As a result, these two have a tendency to burn through their resources together and may find themselves left with nothing if they're not careful. Indecision and poor financial management may be particularly serious problems if they run a business together. However, despite these issues, the overall compatibility between these two signs tends to be high. Their intellectual rapport is great and they can have a lot of fun together.

Libra + Cancer

This can be a difficult match. Although both signs require a partner to feel complete, Libra tends to be a social butterfly, whereas Cancer is a homebody. When Cancers do go out, they usually prefer to spend time outdoors or at a peaceful local venue such as a neighborhood pub, whereas Libras are typically more interested in attending events and meeting new people. Cancer likes to spend plenty of time alone with a partner, and may have difficulty with Libra's desire to maintain friendships and participate in activities outside of the primary relationship (Cancer will be particularly distressed by Libra's tendency to flirt).

Another problem with this pairing is that Libra is unlikely to understand Cancer's desire for emotional support and can be unsympathetic when Cancer is most in need of compassion. Libras swing more toward the intellectual and rational end of the spectrum than its emotional and intuitive side, so they are often bewildered by Cancerian moods and insecurities. Libra also tends to be easy going and careless with money, which can bother pragmatic, security-loving Cancer.

Serious differences in the way these two signs relate to others can also create problems. Cancer prefers to confront issues head on, whereas Libra avoids confrontation at all costs. This can lead to a situation where Cancer nags and provokes while Libra avoids, deceives, or escapes. Another relational problem arises from the fact that Libras seek egalitarian relationships, whereas Cancers typically prefer to either take care of others or have others take care of them. As a result, Libra may find Cancer too bossy or needy, while Cancer finds Libra cold and uncaring.

This combination does have some positive features (though it works best if other elements in their natal zodiacs bring their temperaments into better alignment). Libra tends to be diplomatic, which reduces the risk of accidentally causing emotional harm to sensitive Cancer, and Cancer is nurturing, which can extend to the creation of a beautiful and harmonious home that Libra is bound to appreciate.

Libra + Leo

This is a great combination, both for friendship and romance. These two tend to get along well because Libra appreciates Leo's decisiveness and strength of character, and Leo loves Libra's wit, charm, and style. However, Leo might find Libra a bit too easy going or even weak (Leos respect Leonine traits such as forcefulness and dominance, even though they find them difficult to live with in another person). This lack of respect for Libran mellowness could reduce the potency of a romantic relationship, but for the most part, these two are well-matched and often share common interests and lifestyle preferences.

Both signs have a decadent streak, so they may bond over the pursuit of luxury. These two friendly, extroverted individuals can also have a great social life together because both love to get out, meet people, and be admired. In addition, they share a strong romantic streak, which is beneficial for serious relationships. On the other hand, both tend to fall in love with idealized versions of their partners rather than their real selves, which can lead to disappointment. To make matters worse, they also tend to fall in love with the idea of being love, but may have difficulty with the duller or more difficult day-to-day aspects of living with others once the initial bloom of passion has faded.

Although both Leo and Libra like a lot of attention, Libras are usually happy to let Leos be the leaders and the centers of attention (or at least let them think that they are), which helps to prevent conflicts. Libras are tolerant and egalitarian by nature, so they don't try to dominate their partners. This means that Libra is less likely to threaten Leo's sense of power and control. Libra is also not inclined to pick fights, which can keep things harmonious. However, some Leos may see their Libra partners' efforts to keep things calm and smooth as a lack of passion. On the other hand, Libran tact and diplomacy reduce the risk that Leo's ego will be punctured by a careless word or sharp criticism.

There are some differences in the ways that Leo and Libra perceive the world, which can cause misunderstandings. Leos run on emotion, while Libras process things intellectually. Loyal, emotional Leos passionately defend those they care about, while detached, reasonable Libras can see both sides of an issue and tend to make their judgments based on fairness rather than favoritism. This may lead to problems if Leo demands that Libra take a side in a conflict but Libra stubbornly maintains a rational, neutral stance. If Leo perceives Libra as disloyal, this can be a deal breaker. However, if these two can meet each other halfway, with Leo making an effort to understand other perspectives and Libra showing absolute loyalty in particularly sensitive situations, their differing views of conflict are unlikely to create serious problems.

Libra + Virgo

These two signs aren't bad together. Both tend to be fastidious and intellectually focused. Virgo is not particularly possessive and so can better tolerate Libra's flirting than those of many other signs, and Libra can tolerate Virgo's exacting fussiness because Libras tend to set high standards for themselves as well (also, they are not inclined to quibble over details, so they tend to let Virgos have their way). Both signs are inclined to be diplomatic and they share an intense dislike of conflict, which reduces the likelihood of fights. However, there are significant differences in lifestyle preferences and the ways in which these two signs relate to the world that may create problems.

Libras tend to be highly sociable. They enjoy mixing with others and sharing ideas. Although Virgos also seek the intellectual stimulation of discussion and debate, they are quick to tire of the endless rounds of socializing that Libras usually prefer and have little patience for gatherings where small talk is the norm. The typical Libra could happily spend every night at a party or a pub, or in some other venue with friends and plenty of new people to mix things up. The typical Virgo, on the other hand, needs plenty of time alone to recharge and prefers smaller gatherings of long-time companions to a raucous crowd. Social orientations will be brought into better alignment if the Libra has a more introverted rising sign or the Virgo has a more gregarious ascendant.

Libras are also romantic idealists, which can clash with Virgo's tendency toward practical realism (sensible Virgo may burst Libra's bubbles of optimism from time to time). Another potential source of conflict between these two signs is that Libra is more likely to be open-minded and non-judgemental, while Virgo is more inclined to be skeptical and to form strong opinions. Also, Libras crave flattery and crumble under criticism, and Virgos can be quite direct (and they are not inclined to stroke egos). This can lead to a situation where Libra is easily charmed by someone else who is more complimentary, or Virgo leaves in search of someone who requires less bolstering.

Another problem with this pairing is that Libra likes to spend money on a good time (and on looking good), while Virgo tends to be more practical and cautious with money. In a worst-case scenario, Virgo will find Libra shallow, frivolous, and self-indulgent, while Libra finds Virgo uptight and repressive. However, in a best-case scenario, Libra will pick up some of Virgo's common sense, and Virgo's hidden sensuality will be brought to the surface by Libra's warm, affectionate nature. This pair will always have lots of interesting things to talk about and they will probably find one another's minds fascinating, even if living together requires a significant amount of compromise.

Libra + Libra

Two Libras are likely to get along well and enjoy a great intellectual rapport, though the relationship might not make progress due to mutual indecision. Otherwise, this tolerant, compromising duo should be very compatible and have a smooth and easy time of it whether they have paired up for romance, friendship, or a business partnership (unless other elements in their natal zodiacs are highly unfavorable). Neither is inclined to fight (in fact, both will avoid conflict like the plague unless their ascendants fall in more combative signs), so major clashes are unlikely. When Libras do argue, they tend to pull their verbal punches to avoid doing serious damage. Neither will be inclined to dominate the other and both will seek to establish a balanced relationship of equals, which reduces the risk of strife. If these two do part ways, it will more likely be due to boredom or the desire for a stronger partner than as a result of serious conflict.

Typical Libras want to be in a partnership at all times, and they usually devote a lot of energy to their relationships. However, they also understand one another's need to pursue friendships and opportunities for personal development outside the primary relationship (and perhaps flirt with others a little from time to time for the ego boost).

Neither is inclined to be clingy and both like to get out and mingle.

One potential risk with a Libra-Libra romantic pairing is that many Libras are drawn to strong, decisive partners who can take the lead so that they never have to. Also, although the Libra-Libra combination tends to be pleasant and intellectually stimulating, it may also lack passion and intensity, so there is a risk of boredom in a romantic pairing. In addition, Libras have such a strong desire to be liked and to keep things perfect (at least on the surface) that they are unlikely to bring up contentious issues. This means that when two Libras pair up, they may never discuss sensitive subjects, leaving unaddressed issues to fester and poison the relationship. However, despite these potential problems, this tends to be a positive match. These two are likely to have shared interests, a great social life, and plenty of fun together.

Libra + Scorpio

This is a very powerful connection, emotionally rewarding and passionate in romance, but there can be some problems with this pairing. Although Libra will find Scorpio's intense focus initially flattering in a romantic relationship, Scorpio's jealousy combined with Libra's tendency to flirt can be a volatile mix.

Scorpios and Libras have very different ways of perceiving and making sense of the world. The Libra approach tends to be fair, balanced, and detached, while Scorpios are fiercely loyal, one-sided, and emotionally involved. Scorpios follow their gut instincts while Libras look at things from a rational perspective. There is no right or wrong here, only a difference of styles, and both signs could benefit from adopting each other's approaches in situations that warrant them (following gut instincts could make Libra more decisive, and calmly weighing the pros and cons of a situation could help Scorpio become less reactive).

There are also differences in the ways in which these two signs interact with the world. Scorpios tend to be secretive and somewhat introverted. They are driven by obsessive interests and spend a lot of time pursuing personal goals and engaging in private activities. Libras take a lighter approach to life; they may abandon hobbies or interests because they grow bored and they have a much higher need to socialize with others on a daily basis. As a result, these two may clash over preferred activities and general lifestyle choices, and there is also a risk that Scorpio will view Libra as frivolous and shallow, while Libra finds Scorpio demanding, controlling, and somewhat frightening.

Problems may also arise due to the different ways in which these signs prefer to deal with conflict. Scorpio likes to address things head on, while Libra avoids strife at all costs. This can lead to a situation where Scorpio attacks; Libra retreats, gives in, or even deceives to avoid a fight; and nothing ever gets resolved.

Despite the potential problems associated with this pairing, it does have a number of strengths as well. In a positive relationship, Libra will appreciate Scorpio's strength and decisiveness and Scorpio will be calmed by Libra's peaceful nature. Scorpio's passion will maintain Libra's interest, and Libra's more laid back approach to life will help Scorpio lighten up a bit as well. But whether this connection is beautiful of disastrous will likely depend on other factors in their two natal zodiacs. This match works best when these two individuals have more compatible ascendants and moon signs.

Libra + Sagittarius

This is a fun connection for friendship or romance, though it may lack staying power unless these two have their moons or ascendants in earth signs (such as Taurus or Capricorn) or water signs (such as Cancer or Scorpio) to give the match more depth and stability. The Libra-Sagittarius pairing is playful and intellectually stimulating, and these two signs tend to get along well. However, both are typically so laid back that one or the other may drift off in search of something new, and there is also a risk that Libra might not get the desired relationship security from Sagittarius in a romantic partnership.

Libra and Sagittarius will usually enjoy one another's company immensely. Also, both tend to be extroverted, so neither is likely to demand a quiet evening at home if the other suggests a night out with friends (or strangers). This pair can have a great social life together.

Libra will enjoy the Sagittarian adventurousness, perhaps a little too much at times. Easy-going, open-minded Libra won't put the brakes on Sagittarius's more unrealistic schemes. As a result, these two can get into a lot of trouble together or end up broke, though they'll probably have a lot of fun along the way. Both signs have a tendency toward optimism, and overconfident Sagittarius may take Libra on a ride to financial ruin or some other disaster because Libra tends to cheerfully go along with others for the experience.

Settling down can become an issue in romantic Libra-Sagittarius pairings because Libras have a strong need for partnership while Sagittarians always have their eyes on the horizon. Libra may seek a commitment sooner than Sagittarius is ready to make it, though probably not in a clingy or demanding way. If this pair do settle down together, Libra will give Sagittarius the freedom to pursue separate interests and friendships, so Sagittarius is less likely to feel trapped and seek a means of escape.

One point of contention with these two is that typical Libras like to maintain tidy, attractive homes, whereas typical Sagittarians are not particularly domestic, so they may disagree on household issues. However, Sagittarius tends to cheerfully ignore complaints and Libra will usually let things go rather than picking fights about them, so these different domestic styles are unlikely to create serious problems for this pair.

Libra + Capricorn

These two may be drawn together because Libra finds Capricorn's strength and classiness appealing and Capricorn appreciates Libra's social skills and intellectual interests, but this can be a difficult combination unless other elements in their natal zodiacs are very compatible. Lifestyles and attitudes are poles apart, and there is a risk that Libra will find Capricorn dull and overly cautious, and that Capricorn will find Libra flighty and frivolous. These problems are unlikely to trigger noisy fights because both signs tend to be diplomatic and they share a hatred of ugly scenes, but a smoldering resentment may develop, with Libra dismissing Capricorn as gloomy and depressing and Capricorn assuming that Libra is shallow and self-absorbed.

A major problem with this pairing is that these two interact with the world in very different ways. Capricorns tend to be more introverted. They do socialize, but they're very selective about their companions and prefer to confine their friendships to a smaller number of trusted individuals. Typical Libras have a need to get out and meet new people on a regular basis, and they're far more interested in entertaining different perspectives.

Another point of divergence between these two is that Capricorns tend to put more emphasis on achieving goals and becoming successful, whereas Libras are more inclined to seek social connectedness and the enjoyment of life's more decadent pleasures (which Capricorn will probably view as laziness). In addition, Capricorns tend to be more active and hardworking, whereas Libras can become indolent if they can get away with it (though their vanity will usually motivate them to exercise, their friendliness may draw them into team sports, and their love of luxury will often encourage them to excel at work in pursuit of higher incomes).

There are also differences in the ways in which Capricorns and Libras perceive the world. Libras tend to be idealistic, while Capricorns are inclined toward realism or even pessimism. The typical Capricorn is slow to trust and warm up to others due to a rather cynical view of human nature and is not inclined to be exceptionally romantic, even within a romantic relationship. As a result, Capricorn may be perceived as cold and distant by Libra, who craves affection and regular declarations of love.

This match will have more staying power if these two can benefit from one another's complementary traits and learn to compromise in day-to-day life. In a best-case scenario, Libra will help Capricorn relax and enjoy life more, and Capricorn will provide direction and stability for Libra.

Capricorn can create a solid home base and take care of the practical aspects of life while Libra does the work of cultivating a broader range of friendships for the couple and maintaining these social ties. This match has more potential if other elements in their natal zodiacs bring their temperaments into better alignment.

Libra + Aquarius

Libra and Aquarius usually get along well and understand one another on a deeper level. They enjoy a great intellectual rapport and should have a harmonious relationship because although both like to debate, neither is inclined toward fighting over emotionally charged issues unless their ascendants fall in more combative signs. In fact, both prefer to live in their heads and process things rationally rather than through the distorting lens of feelings.

The rapport between Libra and Aquarius tends to be easy and laid back, which is great for day-to-day living, though this match may lack passion in a romantic relationship unless other elements in their natal zodiacs provide some sparks. However, the conversation should be great and these two are likely to share some interests, creating common ground over which to bond. If a deeper relationship develops, it is more likely to resemble a solid friendship with bedroom privileges than a stormy romance with an inevitable expiry date.

Both Libra and Aquarius tend to be quite sociable, but Aquarians are more inclined to use their social time productively by joining groups involved in charitable or political activities or working with others to do or produce something. This activity-focused socializing can inspire Libra to take up new causes and activities as well. Libras, in turn, have the diplomatic skills required to gently steer Aquarians away from some of their more crazy or detrimental pursuits without being perceived as oppressive. This is important, because Aquarians are fiercely freedom-oriented and stubborn, and they resent those who tell them what to do. Libras are skilled at persuading others without making them feel as though they're being ordered about, which is a much-needed ability in a relationship with an Aquarius.

Libra and Aquarius will usually give one another the social freedom each requires, allowing for friendships and hobbies outside the primary romantic partnership. Libras are more relationship-oriented than Aquarians, who tend to spread their energies among a wider circle of people even when sexually faithful. However, this shouldn't be a deal breaker, as Libras are very good at understanding and accommodating other people's perspectives and allowing them the space they need to pursue their own interests. Overall this is a highly compatible match for friendship and romance.

Libra + Pisces

This can be a fairytale romance or a nightmare, a beautiful friendship or a social disaster, but it will likely fall to one extreme or the other. Although these two signs can irritate each another, they also have plenty in common. Both tend to be romantic, creative, idealistic, aesthetically inclined, and peace seeking. Both crave harmony and avoid emotional conflict whenever possible. However, there are also some fundamental differences between these two signs that can create problems.

Pisces tends to run on intuition and emotion, while Libra favors logic and rationality. This can result in Pisces perceiving Libra as cold and only shallowly connected to others, while Libra views Pisces as irrational and emotionally draining. This pairing works best when other elements in their natal zodiacs bring their psychological styles into better alignment.

Libra and Pisces also tend to have different lifestyle preferences. Pisceans need plenty of time alone to recharge their batteries, whereas Libras want lots of time with their partners and other people. Libra's need to get out and be with others on a frequent basis may make Pisces feel insecure, while the Piscean desire for emotional reassurance may irritate Libra, who has little patience for emotional neediness.

Perhaps the most serious problem with this pairing is that both individuals tend to admire strong, decisive companions and neither can provide this for the other unless their ascendants fall in more solid signs such as Aries, Taurus, Leo, Scorpio, or Capricorn. Each may look to the other to take the lead in a crisis situation and neither may volunteer.

Despite the problems with this pairing, it does have some strengths. Both signs need a peaceful home life to be mentally healthy, and both are inclined to compromise and try to understand the perspectives of others rather than demanding that others convert to their own points of view. This increases the likelihood that these two can live together without major clashes. They are also inclined to find one another's minds interesting, so they are unlikely to grow bored with each other. If other elements in their natal zodiacs are compatible, this match has potential.

Chapter 4: Libra Marriage

Traditional astrological wisdom holds that Libras are most compatible with Gemini, Leo, Libra Sagittarius, and Aquarius, and least compatible with Aries, Cancer, Capricorn, and Pisces. But what do the actual marriage and divorce statistics say?

Mathematician Gunter Sachs (1998) conducted a large-scale study of sun signs, encompassing nearly one million people in Switzerland, which found statistically significant results on a number of measures including marriage and divorce. Castille (2000) conducted a similar study in France using marriage statistics collected between 1976 and 1997, which included more than six million marriages. Findings from these studies are summarized below.

The following pages provide an overall ranking from most common to least common marriages with Libra men and women (* indicates that the result is statistically significant—in other words, the rate was much higher or lower than could be attributed to random chance).

Libra Men: Marriage Rates

Sachs study

1. Libra*
2. Leo
3. Gemini
4. Cancer
5. Sagittarius
6. Capricorn
7. Virgo
8. Aquarius
9. Taurus
10. Pisces
11. Aries (tied with Pisces)
12. Scorpio

Castile study

1. Libra*
2. Virgo
3. Leo
4. Sagittarius
5. Scorpio
6. Pisces
7. Aries
8. Taurus
9. Capricorn
10. Aquarius
11. Gemini
12. Cancer

Libra Women: Marriage Rates

Sachs study

1. Taurus*
2. Libra*
3. Gemini
4. Virgo
5. Scorpio
6. Leo
7. Aries
8. Aquarius
9. Sagittarius
10. Capricorn
11. Cancer
12. Pisces*

Castille study

1. Libra*
2. Sagittarius
3. Leo
4. Scorpio
5. Virgo
6. Gemini
7. Aries
8. Taurus
9. Aquarius
10. Capricorn
11. Pisces*
12. Cancer*

Some Notes on Marriage Rates

In keeping with traditional astrological wisdom, both Sachs and Castille found that two Libras often make a good match, with higher-than-average rates of marriage. Libras are inclined to avoid conflict at all costs, so serious fights between two Libras are unlikely. Both also have a strong aesthetic appreciation, a love of refinement, and a need for domestic harmony that helps to keep things peaceful.

Sachs found that Libra women are even more likely to marry Taurus men than Libra men, and there is a good foundation for the Libra-Taurus match. While there are some differences between the two signs in terms of personality and perspective, both are laid back and not inclined toward argument, and they share a love of domestic harmony and a need for comfortable and beautiful surroundings. Libra women will appreciate Taurean strength and decisiveness, while Tauruses value Libran refinement and class. A particular benefit with this pairing is that accommodating Libras are less likely to provoke the infamous Taurean stubbornness.

As for the pairings that occur with a less-than-average frequency, seeing Cancer at the bottom of the list is no surprise, given that Libra and Cancer tend to clash unless their ascendants or moon signs are more compatible. Libra flirtatiousness may make Cancer feel insecure, and Libra may find Cancer too moody and quick to take offense. Being highly sensitive by nature, Cancers may pick fights in response to minor or imagined slights, and Libras abhor conflict. Also, Cancers like to force emotional issues out into the open, whereas Libras prefer to avoid emotionally charged conversations, which can lead to a breakdown in communication.

Sachs also found that Libra women are least likely to marry Pisces men, and Castile found a lower-than-average rate of marriage for Libra women and Pisces men as well. Given that Pisces is known for emotional intensity while Libra craves stability, rationality, and balance, it's no surprise that these two face challenges unless other elements in their natal zodiacs are more compatible. Typical Pisceans are too intense and chaotic for Libras, though this match can work if other elements in their natal zodiacs are better aligned.

Divorce

The Sachs study also provides insights into which romantic matches are most likely to stick. The following are statistically significant findings for divorce rates (in other words, effects too big to attribute to random chance).

As would be expected, Libra men divorced Aries women more frequently than those of any other sign. Aries deals with issues by tackling them head on, whereas Libra detests arguments. This can lead to a situation in which Aries provokes and Libra gives in or retreats. Communication breakdown can result. The study also found that Libra men were least likely to divorce Libra women. This is an expected result, given that two Libras are fundamentally compatible.

Libra women were also least likely to divorce Libra men and most likely to divorce Leo men. Although Leo is theoretically a compatible sign, Libra's flirtatiousness and Leo's need to be the center of attention may not always mix well in a romantic relationship. As for divorce, Sachs found that Libra women are least likely to divorce Libra men.

Note: Even if your partnership falls into one of the higher-than-average divorce rate categories, that doesn't mean it's doomed to failure. The sun sign is only one element in a natal zodiac that determines compatibility, and there may be other elements in your natal zodiacs that make you far more compatible than would be expected based on sun signs alone.

The Best Romantic Match for Libra

In keeping with traditional astrological wisdom, Sachs found that two Libras often make a good match, with higher-than-average rates of marriage and lower-than-average rates of divorce. Libras are inclined to avoid conflict at all costs, so serious fights between two Libras are unlikely. Both have a strong aesthetic appreciation, a love of refinement, and a need for domestic harmony that helps to keep things peaceful.

The best match for Libras of either gender appears to be another Libra, whereas Aries is a particularly incompatible match for Libra men, and Cancer, Leo, and Pisces are particularly difficult for Libra women. However, Libras who find themselves romantically entangled with one of the less compatible signs should not despair. Plenty of marriages between supposedly incompatible signs have lasted.

It's important to keep in mind that these are statistical tendencies; this doesn't mean that every romance between incompatible signs is doomed. For example, out of 6,498,320 marriages encompassing all possible sign combinations in the Castille study, there were 922 *more* marriages between Libra women and Libra men than would be expected if sun signs had no effect, whereas between Libra women and Cancer men, there were 465 *fewer* marriages than would be expected if pairings were random. However, there still were many marriages between the supposedly least compatible signs.

Astrology is complex, and there is more to consider than just sun signs. Two people with incompatible sun signs may have highly compatible rising signs or moon signs that can make the difference between a bad match and a good match with a bit of an "edge" that keeps things interesting.

*The Sachs study has been criticized for not taking potential confounding variables into account and continues to be controversial. I have found no critiques of the Castille study thus far.

Chapter 5: Why Some Signs Are More Compatible With Libra Than Others

Why are some astrological signs considered more or less compatible with Libra than others? Traditional astrologers believe that signs of the same element will be the most compatible, and that fire and air signs will be more compatible with one another, as will earth and water signs, whereas fire and air are more likely to clash with earth and water. They also believe that clashes are more likely to occur among different signs of the same quality (cardinal, fixed, or mutable).

Compatibility according to traditional astrologers:

- Libra (air, cardinal) + Aries (fire, cardinal): very challenging
- Libra (air, cardinal) + Taurus (earth, fixed): somewhat challenging
- Libra (air, cardinal) + Gemini (air, mutable): Excellent
- Libra (air, cardinal) + Cancer (water, cardinal): very challenging
- Libra (air, cardinal) + Leo (fire, fixed): good
- Libra (air, cardinal) + Virgo (earth, mutable): somewhat challenging
- Libra (air, cardinal) + Libra (air, cardinal): excellent
- Libra (air, cardinal) + Scorpio (water, fixed): somewhat challenging
- Libra (air, cardinal) + Sagittarius (fire, mutable): good
- Libra (air, cardinal) + Capricorn (earth, cardinal): very challenging
- Libra (air, cardinal) + Aquarius (air, fixed): excellent
- Libra (air, cardinal) + Pisces (water, mutable): somewhat challenging

The Elements

The astrological elements are fire, earth, air, and water. Each element includes three of the twelve astrological signs.

Fire Signs: Aries, Leo, Sagittarius

Those who have a lot of planets in fire signs tend to be courageous, enterprising, and confident. Their love of excitement causes them take risks, and they are often extravagant or careless with money.

Fire people are generous to a fault, idealistic, and helpful. They are quick to anger, but also quick to forgive, and usually honest, in many cases to the point of bluntness or tactlessness.

Fire people are energetic and often athletic. They are assertive and (in some cases) aggressive or argumentative. Impulsivity can lead to poor decisions, financial disasters, and unnecessary conflict. Extroverted and easily bored, they seek attention and tend to be affectionate and friendly.

Earth Signs: Taurus, Virgo, Capricorn

Those who have many planets in earth signs tend to be responsible, reliable, and trustworthy. They can usually be counted on to provide stability and practical help, and they are loyal to their friends and not inclined to be fickle, though when someone crosses them, they can be quite ruthless in cutting that person out of their lives forever. Slow to anger but equally slow to forgive, they often hold grudges. However, they are usually reasonable and diplomatic unless severely provoked.

People whose natal zodiacs are weighted toward earth signs tend to be physically strong and have great endurance. They are inclined to achieve success through hard work, and their innate cautiousness, fear of change, and need for security keep them from making rash decisions or gambling excessively, though these traits can also cause them to miss opportunities or get into ruts. While not exceptionally innovative, they have good follow-through and are able to finish what they start.

Air Signs: Gemini, Libra, Aquarius

Those who have a lot of planets in air signs are intellectual rather than emotional, which can cause some to view them as insensitive, though they tend to be friendly and sociable. Logical, rational, and emotionally detached by nature, they can be open-minded and non-judgmental in most cases.

People whose natal zodiacs are weighted toward air signs are adaptable, mentally flexible, and easy going. They rarely blow up at others in anger-provoking situations, as they are more inclined to analyze circumstances than to react passionately. They are also easily bored and require a diverse array of social companions, hobbies, and other entertainments.

Air people usually love change and tend to be experimental and open to new experiences. Impulsivity and curiosity can cause them to make impractical decisions or squander their money.

Water Signs: Cancer, Scorpio, Pisces

Those who have many planets in water signs are highly intuitive, which enables them to discern the emotions, needs, and motivations of others. They are compassionate and inclined to care for the physically sick and the emotionally damaged, self-sacrificing on behalf of those they care for, and even in the service of strangers in some cases.

Sensitive and easily hurt, many water people develop a tough outer shell to hide their vulnerability. They are passionate in their attachments to people and prone to jealousy. Because they are idealistic, they often gloss over the faults of others, so they can be deceived by unscrupulous people.

Water people are sensual and creative. Given the right environment and opportunity, they can produce art, music, literature, or in some cases, inventions or scientific ideas that have profound effects on others.

The Qualities

The astrological qualities are fixed, cardinal, and mutable. Each category includes four of the astrological signs.

Cardinal: Aries, Cancer, Libra, Capricorn

A person with the majority of natal planets in cardinal signs will be enterprising and inclined to initiate courses of action. Cardinal people make things happen and transform situations. This can be done for the benefit or detriment of others.

Fixed: Taurus, Leo, Scorpio, Aquarius

Those who have a lot of planets in fixed signs have good follow-through. They tend to stick to a single course of action and carry out activities to their completion or conclusion. Fixed-sign people are often moody or stubborn, and they have intense reactions to things. However, they can act as stabilizing forces for others because they tend to behave in a consistent manner.

Mutable: Gemini, Virgo, Sagittarius, Pisces

Those who have the majority of their planets in mutable signs are flexible and adaptable. They accept change and adjust well to new circumstances that can throw other types off kilter. Mutable people often function better in a crisis than in a stable situation.

See Appendix 3 for information on how to find your other planetary placements to determine which elements and qualities are predominant in your natal zodiac.

Chapter 6: Libra Children

Libra children are usually well behaved and easygoing. They rarely have problems making friends and dealing with new people, and they are more likely to suppress their own needs than to throw a tantrum.

Libra children tend to be neat and tidy, but they may also be lazy daydreamers. They're usually reasonable with others, rarely attempting to take more than their fair share of anything, and they will often stick up for those who are being mistreated, even if the victims are unpopular.

Typical Libra children have sunny, optimistic temperaments and get over most childhood upsets quickly (unless their moon signs incline them toward more depressive temperaments). They are usually well-balanced rather than prone to extremes (for example, they are less likely to belong to a recognizable category, such as nerd, artist, or jock, instead showing a wide range of interests).

Libra children are particularly sensitive to discord, and can become very distressed when family members fight. Ongoing conflicts can make them psychologically or even physically ill.

Libra children may intervene in family arguments as peacemakers from an early age or hide until things have calmed down, and they are less likely than other children to provoke or escalate fights (the exception to this rule is a Libra child whose ascendant or moon is in one of the fire signs: Aries, Leo, or Sagittarius).

Chapter 7: Libra Parents

Libra parents are open-minded, reasonable, and unlikely to shout at their children or humiliate them in public. They take a diplomatic and logical approach to problems and tend to be tolerant and forgiving. There are factors that may modify this, however. A Libra parent with Aries rising will be more confrontational and combative, and a Libra parent with Taurus or Scorpio rising may be more inclined to hold grudges.

The greatest strengths of typical Libra parents are their lack of prejudice, their diplomacy, and their ability to contemplate both sides of an argument or an issue. This allows them to see things from a child's perspective and to come up with fair and reasonable solutions to problems.

Weaknesses afflicting some Libra parents include self-absorption, indecisiveness, and a tendency to crumble under pressure (however, other placements such as Aries, Leo, Scorpio, or Capricorn rising can create a tougher Libra personality). Libra parents may also go through many marriages and divorces due to their exceptionally strong need to find ideal partners, which can be disruptive for children. In addition, some Libra parents are overly concerned with physical appearance (their own or their children's), as well as the appearance of their homes and possessions. However, although a small proportion of Libras can be very selfish or vain, they are rarely vengeful or deliberately cruel.

On the plus side, Libra parents are not likely to dominate their children, force them into certain lifestyles or professions, or try to indoctrinate them into a particular belief system. Libras tend follow a live-and-let-live philosophy and treat others the way they would like to be treated. This tolerant, open-minded attitude is among the positive legacies that Libras can pass on to their children.

Chapter 8: Libra Health and Safety

The Sachs study also provided some insights into Libra tendencies with regard to health and safety. Libras were statistically less likely than those of other signs to commit suicide, in keeping with the optimistic Libra nature and this sign's tendency toward balance rather than extremes. Libras tend to weigh their options and think about the pros and cons rather than acting impulsively, which may reduce their risk of taking such a radical, drastic action. They are more inclined toward rational problem solving than dramatic expressions of despair.

Sachs also found that Libras were slightly more likely to cause car accidents than the average for the twelve sun signs, but were in the middle of the pack for accidents causing serious damage. Overall, the results suggest that they are average drivers in terms of safety, but could be a little more cautious.

According to traditional astrology, health problems associated with the sign of Libra in include kidney, adrenal, and bladder issues; low back pain; skin problems; and fluctuating energy levels. These problems are more likely to occur in response to stress, particularly when Libras find themselves in conflict-ridden situations from which they feel they cannot escape.

To maintain their health, Libras should be very careful in their selection of romantic partners, roommates, friends, and coworkers, as they are particularly vulnerable to becoming ill in response to stress caused by environments where people are regularly fighting. They should also avoid skipping meals, trying fad diets, or eating sugary snacks, as the problem of highly variable energy levels can be exacerbated by blood sugar fluctuations. In addition, Libras need to engage in one or more physical activities on a regular basis, ideally including an activity that helps with mind-body balance, such as yoga, Thai chi, walking, hiking, or swimming outdoors in a lake or ocean.

Chapter 9: Libra Attitudes, Preferences, and Lifestyles

The Sachs study also included market research data to provide insights into the attitudes, hobbies, lifestyles, and consumer behaviors associated with each sun sign.

Preferred Methods of Persuasion

According to the market research data, Libras were more inclined than those of other signs to say they disliked moral or emotion-based arguments and to prefer arguments based on logic and facts. Libra is associated with rationality, logic, and balance, so this finding is in keeping with the traditional astrological profile for this sign.

Tolerance

Libras also rated tolerance for foreigners and those of other faiths as very important to them, which comes as no surprise, given Libra's reputation as a tolerant, open-minded, and diplomatic sign.

Social Status

Libras were less inclined than those of other signs to view a rise in social status as important. Some traditional astrologers have characterized Libras as social climbers, but Libras may actually be more concerned with ideas and intellectual stimulation than status.

Spending

Libras were not inclined to see thrift (saving money by purchasing less expensive items) as important. This finding regarding thrift is in line with traditional astrological characterizations of Libra, as this sign is often associated with frivolity and extravagance.

Attitudes

Libras were less inclined than those of other signs to say there was a large generation gap between their own attitudes and those of their parents. This may be attributable to the fact that moderate, reasonable, conflict-avoidant Libras are more inclined to either agree with others or gravitate to a moderate belief system that is less likely to diverge significantly from the moderate views held by the majority of people.

Balance

Libras rated themselves highly on multidimensional behavior (a balanced range of activities as opposed to an extreme focus on one thing). This is in keeping with traditional astrological views of Libras as well-balanced.

Spirituality

Libras were more inclined to describe themselves as religious, which is interesting in light of the Libra preference for factual over moral arguments. However, Libras may have a strong spiritual side without believing that their religious beliefs conflict with scientific knowledge or feeling a need to impose their belief systems on others.

Personality

Libras were less inclined than those of other signs to rate their personalities as weak. While traditional astrology books sometimes paint the Libra persona as timid or wishy-washy, Libras can be very strong-willed when sticking up for justice, particularly when defending an underdog. It's just that they are more inclined to exhibit this strength of character for the benefit of another individual or group than on their own behalf.

Fashion Sense

Libras showed a preference for dressing in youthful clothing and were slightly more trendy and fashion conscious than the average for the sun signs, as well as being less likely to prefer casual or informal clothing. This is in keeping with the traditional astrological view of Libras as fashion-conscious and well-dressed.

Insurance

Libras were less likely than those of other signs to be the decision makers when it came to buying insurance, in keeping with the fact that this sign is not known for decisiveness or practicality.

Marriage

Libra women rated themselves as less eager to get married than women of most other signs (besides Taurus). This is a surprising finding in light of the fact that Libra is the sign of partnership. However, air sign people tend to value their independence very highly, and Libras often have nearly impossible romantic standards, so the finding may reflect an unwillingness to settle for less rather than disinterest in marriage. Libra women may also prefer to cohabitate rather than rushing into marriage so that they have the opportunity to assess compatibility before making a lifelong commitment.

Chapter 10: Libra Interests, Hobbies, and Leisure Activities

Politics

Data provided by Sachs indicates that Libras are more likely to express an interest in politics than the average for the sun signs. Given that Libra is strongly linked with politics, this comes as no surprise.

Holidays, Property, and Furnishings

Libras also showed a strong interest in holidays and travel and in property and furnishings. Given that Libra is associated with decadence, aesthetics, and leisure, these findings accord with traditional perceptions of the Libra personality as well.

Gardening

Libras were more inclined than those of other signs to have vegetable gardens, perhaps because vegetable gardens provide opportunities to spend time in a peaceful environment, designing and tending something aesthetically pleasing.

European Football (Soccer)

Libras were also more inclined to play European football than those of other signs. Although athletic pursuits requiring more balance and grace such as skating, yoga, or martial arts are often specified as Libra pastimes by traditional astrologers, the outgoing, compromising Libra nature suits this sign to team sports as well.

Libras are good at coordinating their efforts with others to support collective goals and working cooperatively with a group, so it is no surprise that they gravitate to certain team-based athletic pursuits.

Other Interests

Libras were inclined to give advice on large electrical appliances, photography, movies, and product testing. These trends may indicate that Libras often have a specific interest in these topics or simply like to give advice in general. None of these topics are linked with the sign of Libra, though photography and movies do have an aesthetic element. Libras are also among the most enthusiastic shoppers of the zodiac (second only to Leos), which would give them an affinity for product testing.

Hobbies

How well do the market research findings accord with traditional astrological beliefs about Libra pastimes? Hobbies associated with the sign of Libra include:

- Attending art shows, concerts, and parties
- Beautifying (self or surroundings)
- Dancing
- Debate or discussion (particularly politics or philosophy)
- Design and decoration (buildings, interiors, or fashions)
- Entertaining
- Flirting
- Reading
- Shopping
- Sunbathing
- Tai chi
- Team sports (particularly soccer)
- Yoga

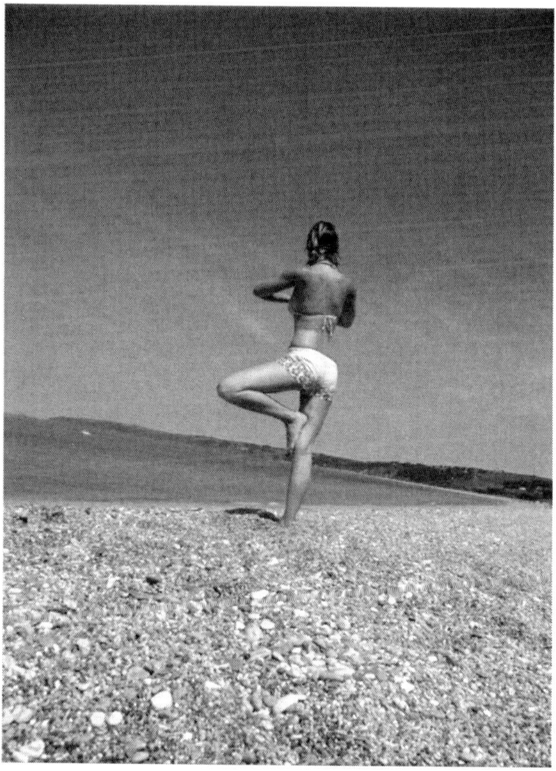

Chapter 11: Libras Behaving Badly

Sachs found that Libras were slightly more likely than those of other signs to be convicted of theft or drug use and less likely to be convicted of driving without a license (these were the only three statistically significant results from the study of sun signs and crime rates). The top three crimes for which Libras were convicted overall included theft, drug use, and embezzlement.

Theft and embezzlement allow criminals to acquire the finer things in life with relative ease and (in most cases) only small risk of physical violence, while drug use is a self-indulgent pastime, in keeping with the traditional characterization of Libra as decadent and pleasure seeking, but not inclined to vicious cruelty (none of the crimes for which Libra had a higher-than-average rate of conviction were violent offenses).

It should be noted that traditional astrologers consider Libra to be among the less criminally inclined signs of the zodiac overall.

Chapter 12: Libra Stuff

Market research data provided by Sachs indicates that Libras are more likely than those of other signs to own a desktop or portable computer or plan to purchase one in the next couple of years. The sign of Libra is linked with technology and modern things in general, so this was an expected finding.

Libras were also more likely to own or say they would purchase women's fashion accessories in the near future. This sign is also linked with beauty, fashion, and vanity, so this finding accords with traditional astrological views as well.

Another finding in line with traditional characterizations of Libra is that Libras were more likely to have recently bought mouthwash than the average for the sun signs. The higher rate of mouthwash purchasing is no surprise, as Libras are particularly hygienic and socially conscious, so they are more likely fear bad breath.

Other things associated with the sign of Libra, both tangible and intangible, include:

- beauty
- design
- diplomacy
- harmony
- Justice
- logic
- mediation
- paintings
- peace
- perfume
- sculpture

Chapter 13: Libra Studies

According to data provided by Sachs, Libras rated themselves as very eager to study and obtain further education, and they were more likely to study law and less likely to study dentistry. This accords with traditional astrological characterizations of Libra as a seeker of knowledge with an interest in further education.

Law is linked to the sign of Libra because Libras have a talent for assessing both sides of an argument and responding thoughtfully and rationally. Their polished speaking skills, superior powers of persuasion, and sense of diplomacy suit them for careers in law, and their attractive, well-groomed appearances are a bonus for this profession.

Dentistry may have less appeal for typical Libras as some are too squeamish for it and even those who aren't might find the profession stressful because many dental patients experience intense fear due to their phobia of dental procedures. Libras are very motivated to please others and be liked by everyone, so they would find these negative reactions particularly traumatic.

Libras seek pleasant, harmonious interactions with others, so they may avoid professions where they have to do unpleasant things to people, even if those things provide benefits. However, another possible problem with dentistry as a profession for Libras is that opportunities for socializing are minimal because patients tend have implements in their mouth most of the time, so this career would have less appeal for such a naturally outgoing sign.

Chapter 14: Libra Careers

Typical Libras have a strong aesthetic sense and an aptitude for various forms of design. Their visual-spatial skills are usually good, so jobs that require arranging things or spatial planning are favored.

Many Libras have a talent for technology, so technology-related professions may appeal to them, though a creative streak suits them to the arts as well. Diplomatic skills and idealism may also encourage some Libras to choose social work, law, and/or politics.

Many Libras possess a natural grace that suits them to particular athletic careers. Naturally charming, they also do well in hospitality industry positions where they greet and interact with the public.

Libras require a harmonious work environment. Argumentative coworkers can cause significant psychological distress, even if the Libra is not directly involved in the conflicts. Careers where Libras are expected to make quick decisions are also a bad idea unless their ascendants fall in more decisive signs, such as Aries, Leo, Scorpio, or Sagittarius.

Careers and career fields traditionally associated with the sign of Libra include:

- architect
- athlete
- beautician
- dancer/dance instructor
- diplomat
- fashion designer
- florist
- hair stylist
- host/hostess
- interior designer/decorator
- judge
- lawyer
- martial arts instructor
- mediator
- model
- painter
- personnel officer
- politician

- professional ice skater
- receptionist/ secretary
- writer (especially poetry; poetic prose; or philosophical, legal, or politically based works)
- yoga instructor

As for the careers Libras actually prefer, data provided by Sachs indicates that Libras are less inclined than those of other signs to be self-employed and more likely to work in white-collar nonexecutive or blue-collar positions. This accords with the traditional astrological characterization of Libras as preferring to work for others or within a group or a partnership rather than taking on all of the responsibilities themselves.

Libras were less likely than those of other signs to go into farming or become general practitioner doctors, dentists, or teachers. They were more inclined to become bakers, tailors, bricklayers, painters, cabinet makers, bank clerks, decorators, interior designers, and hairdressers. Farmers, doctors, dentists, and teachers must deal with unpleasant interactions (sick animals for farmers, distressed people for doctors and dentists, and challenging students for teachers), so it is no surprise that Libras are less likely to favor these career options.

As for the careers that Libras gravitate to in greater numbers, many are associated with fields that most astrology books have ascribed to Libra. Decorating, designing, painting, and hairdressing are all considered Libra fields, and the decorative aspects of baking, cabinet making, and bricklaying also require a strong aesthetic sense, which is a typical Libra strength. And bank clerks require people skills and a polished appearance, which are also Libra attributes.

It should be noted that some Libras will gravitate toward careers not typical for their sign because their ascendants suit them to different occupations.

Appendix 1: Libra Associations

Metal: copper

Gemstones: emerald, rose quartz, rhodonite, sapphire (September), opal (October)

Parts of the Body: kidneys, lower back and spine, adrenal glands

Number: 6

Animals: dove, butterfly, dolphin, whale, lizard

Trees: chestnut, almond, cypress, ash

Colors: pale blue, pink, lavender

Places: Egypt, Japan, Austria, Burma, Tibet, Argentina, Lisbon, Frankfurt, Copenhagen, Vienna, Charleston

Patterns or Design Motifs: damask, batik, floral, all subtle or classic patterns

Plants and Herbs: rose, sweet pea, daffodil, daisy, foxglove, yarrow, pennyroyal, parsley, lily, mint, groundsel, ivy, vine, hydrangea

Foods: potato, apple, chestnut, walnut, artichoke

Appendix 2: Famous Libras

Famous people with the sun in Libra include:

- Al Sharpton
- Aleister Crowley
- Alfred Nobel
- Alicia Silverstone
- Angela Lansbury
- Anne Rice
- Annie Leibovitz
- Annika Sorenstam
- Arthur Rimbaud
- Avril Lavigne
- Barbara Walters
- Bela Lugosi
- Benjamin Netanyahu
- Bil Keane
- Bishop Desmond Tutu
- Bob Geldof
- Bonnie Parker (of Bonnie and Clyde)
- Bret Favre
- Brian Boitano
- Brie Larson
- Brigitte Bardot
- Bruce Springsteen
- Bruno Mars
- Buster Keaton
- Carrie Fisher
- Catherine Zeta-Jones
- Charles Munch
- Charlton Heston
- Cheryl Tiegs
- Chevy Chase
- Christopher Lloyd
- Christopher Reeve
- Chuck Berry
- Chuck Lorre
- Clive Barker
- Clive Owen
- Confucious
- Dakota Johnson
- Dale Earnhardt Jr.
- Dan Gutman
- Dawn French

- Deepak Chopra
- Dizzy Gillespie
- Donna Karan
- Dorothy Johnson Vaughan
- Dr. Joyce Brothers
- Dwight D. Eisenhower
- Ed Sullivan
- Eleanor Roosevelt,
- Elie Wiesel
- Elisabeth Shue
- Elmore Leonard
- Emily Deschanel
- Emily Post
- Eminem
- Enrico Ferme
- Eric Stoltz
- Evander Holyfield
- F. Scott Fitzgerald
- Felicity Jones
- Fran Drescher
- Fred West
- Friedrich Nietzsche
- George Gershwin
- George Peppard
- Glenn Gould
- Gore Vidal
- Graham Greene
- Groucho Marx
- Guillermo del Toro
- Guy Pearce
- Gwen Stefani
- Gwyneth Paltrow
- Harvey Washington Wiley
- Heather Locklear
- Hilary Duff
- Hugh Jackman
- Jackie Collins
- Jackson Browne
- James Bevel
- James Caviezel
- James Herriot
- Jean Claude Van Damme
- Jeff Goldblum
- Jesse Eisenberg
- Jesse Jackson
- Jim Henson
- Jimmy Carter

- John Lennon
- John Mellencamp
- Johnny Carson
- Johnny Mathis
- Johnny Ramone
- Josh Hutcherson
- Judge Judy Sheindlin
- Julie Andrews
- Julio Inglesias
- Kate Winslet
- Katherine Mansfield
- Kelly Preston
- Kelly Ripa
- Kevin Durant
- Kim Kardashian
- Kirk Cameron
- Kublai Khan
- Lee Harvey Oswald
- Lee Iacocca
- Lena Headey
- Lil Wayne
- Lillian Gish
- Lindsey Vonn
- Luciano Pavarotti
- Luke Perry
- Ma Barker
- Mae C. Jemison
- Mahatma Gandhi
- Margaret Thatcher
- Marie Osmond
- Mario Lemieux
- Mario Lopez
- Mario Puzo
- Marion Cotillard
- Mark Hamill
- Martina Navratilova
- Matt Damon
- Meatloaf
- Michael Douglas
- Michael Morpurgo
- Michel Foucault
- Mickey Mantle
- Mickey Rooney
- Miguel de Cervantes
- Mike Judge
- Mira Sorvino
- Monica Bellucci
- Montgomery Clift

- Nana Mouskouri
- Nancy Kerrigan
- Naomi Watts
- Neil deGrasse Tyson
- Neve Campbell
- Nick Cannon
- Oliver North
- Olivia Newton John
- Oscar Wilde
- Paul Simon
- Penny Marshall
- Phil Hartman
- Piper Kerman
- Pope Paul VI
- R.L. Stine
- Ralph Lauren
- Ray Charles
- Ray Kroc
- Rex Reed
- Rita Hayworth
- Roger Moore
- Ronald McNair
- Ryan Reynolds
- Sacha Baron Cohen
- Samuel Taylor Coleridge
- Sarah Ferguson
- Scott Baio
- Scott Bakula
- Sean Lennon
- Serena Williams
- Shaun Cassidy
- Shel Silverstein
- Sigourney Weaver
- Simon Cowell
- Snoop Dogg
- Stephanie Zimbalist
- Sting
- Susan Sarandon
- Suzanne Somers
- Thelonious Monk
- Theresa May
- Thomas Wolfe
- Tim Robbins
- Tito Jackson
- Tom Petty
- Tommy Lee
- Ursula K. Le Guin
- Usher

- Viggo Mortensen
- Vladimir Putin
- Walter Lippmann
- Walter Matthau
- Will Smith
- William Faulkner
- Wynton Marsalis
- Zac Efron
- Zach Galifianakis
- Ziggy Marley

Libra Rising (Libra Ascendant)

The ascendant is the mask we wear in social situations, or the outer persona we show to others. In the case of Libra rising, the external personality will be defined by Libra traits, or a blend between Libra and the sun sign.

Famous people with Libra rising include:

- Albert Schweitzer
- Anne Heche
- Bill Clinton
- Britney Spears
- David Bowie
- Dolly Parton
- Eric Clapton
- Francois Mitterand
- Freddie Prinze Jr.
- George Harrison
- Igor Stravinsky
- Isaac Newton
- Jacques Cousteau
- Jane Fonda
- Jennifer Anniston
- John F. Kennedy
- Jon Bon Jovi
- Louis Pasteur
- Neil Diamond
- Pierre Cardin
- Richard Chamberlain
- Rod Stewart
- Sidney Poitier
- Twiggy

Appendix 3: Moon Signs, Ascendants (Rising Signs), and Other Planets

The natal zodiac is like a snapshot of the sky at the moment of birth. Astrologers believe that planetary placements and aspects at the time of birth influence personality and fortune. The sun, moon, and ascendant (rising sign) are the primary astrological forces, though planets also play a role.

Astrodienst (www.Astro.com) offers free chart calculation, so you can use this site to find your planetary placements and aspects and your rising sign (for the rising sign, you will need your time of birth as well as the date and place).

The Most Significant Astrological Forces

Most people know their Sun sign, which is the zodiac position of the sun at the time of birth, but few know their rising or moon signs or where their angular planets lie. In fact, the majority of people are surprised to learn that they even have these things.

Of the planetary placements, the sun, moon, and rising signs have the strongest effect on personality. The other planetary placements (positions of the planets at the time of birth) also have effects, though these are not as strong and tend to be concentrated in certain areas rather than shaping the entire personality.

The Sun Sign: The sun sign provides information about basic character and a framework for the rest of the natal zodiac. However, other elements such as the rising sign (also known as the ascendant) and moon sign affect the way the sun sign is expressed.

The Rising Sign (Ascendant): The rising sign determines the outward expression of personality, or the way in which a person interacts with the external world. It can be described as the public persona or mask. It also indicates how an individual is likely to be perceived by others (how he or she comes across socially).

When the sun and ascendant are in the same or similar signs, a person behaves in a way that is consistent with his or her inner character. When the rising sign is very different from the sun sign, the individual is likely to be pulled in competing directions or to send out signals that don't match inner feelings, which increases the likelihood of being misunderstood by others. While such conflicts can make life difficult, they are also a source of creativity and a spur to achievement.

The Moon Sign: The moon sign is the private persona, only seen in adulthood by those very close to the person. The moon rules over childhood and people are more likely to express their moon sign personalities when they are young. In adulthood, the moon's influence is usually hidden, relegated to the secret emotional life, though an individual may openly express the moon sign persona in times of stress or other emotional extremes.

The moon also represents the mother and other female forces in a person's life. The placement of the moon in a natal chart can indicate the types of relationships and interactions a person is likely to have with women.

Other Planets

Other planets also play a role in shaping the qualities that make up an individual. Each of the planets has a particular sphere of influence, and its effects will be determined by the sign in which the planet falls and the aspects it makes to other planets.

Mercury: all forms of mental activity and communication, including speaking and writing, the intellect, intelligence, reason, perception, memory, understanding, assimilation of information, and critical thinking

Venus: love, affection, pleasure, beauty, sex appeal, art, romantic affairs, adornment, social graces, harmony, and friendship

Mars: physical energy, will power, temper, assertiveness, boldness, competitiveness, impulsiveness, forcefulness, aggression, action, accidents, destructiveness, courage, and sex drive

Jupiter: luck and fortune, optimism, generosity, expansiveness, success, higher education, law, medicine, philosophy, abundance, and spirituality

Saturn: hard work, responsibility, character, strength of will, endurance, hard karma, difficulties, obstacles, hardship, the ability to see a task through to completion, authority, diligence, limitations, self-control, stability, patience, maturity, restriction, and realism

Uranus: progressiveness, change, originality, invention, innovation, technology, science, rebellion, revolution, sudden events and opportunities, awakenings, shocks, flashes of genius, eccentricity, unconventionality, unusual circumstances or events, independence, visionary ideas, and occult interests

Neptune: imagination, intuition, mysticism, dreams, fantasies, compassion, psychic abilities, visions, spirituality, strange events, the subconscious, repressed memories, glamour, mystery, insanity, drama, addiction, ideals, inspiration, transcendence, artistic sensibilities, and creative genius

Pluto: power, transformation, release of dormant forces, change, the subconscious, suppressed energies, death, rebirth, regeneration, sex, jealousy, passion, obsession, intensity, creation and destruction, beginnings and endings that occur simultaneously (one thing ending so that another can begin), secrets, mystery, undercurrents, precognition, personal magnetism, and extremes of personality

House Placements

House placements are a sort of fine tuning, adding some small, specific details about the ways in which various planetary placements will be expressed. The planets represent the spheres of life in which the sign traits are acted out, and the house placements are the stage or setting for these acts.

1st House: self-awareness and self-expression, outer personality, responses to outside stimuli, assertiveness, competitiveness, self-promotion, and courses of action chosen (ruled by mars)

2nd House: material possessions and attitude towards material possessions and money, ability to earn money, extensions of material wealth such as quality of food, decadence, luxury, and physical or external beauty (ruled by Venus)

3rd House: logical and practical reasoning, the intellect, agility, dexterity, curiosity, all forms of communication, all forms of media, intuition about trends and public desires or tendencies, short journeys, and siblings (ruled by Mercury)

4th House: home and hearth, domestic life, domestic chores, family, babies, comfort, the mothering instinct, food, and household items (ruled by the moon)

5th House: creative self-expression, socializing, children, early education, sports, the arts (especially the performing arts), pleasure and places of amusement, parties, social popularity, amd fame (ruled by the sun)

6th House: necessary tasks, details, health consciousness, nutrition, humility, hard work, organization, service, self-control, and sense of duty (ruled by Mercury)

7th House: relationships, friendships, marriage, all forms of partnership (business and social), harmony, balance, conflict avoidance, sense of justice, ideals, the reactions of others to our actions, what attracts us to other people (the sign at the beginning of our seventh house is often the astrological sign we find most attractive), fairness, and aesthetic sense (ruled by Venus)

8th House: legacies, shared resources, taxes, power, death, rebirth, sexuality, the dark side of life, deep psychology, personal magnetism, transformation (self-initiated or imposed by external forces), secrets or secret societies, spying, and prophetic dreaming (ruled by Pluto)

9th House: long distance travel, higher education, religion, medicine, law, animals, knowledge gained through travel and philosophical thinking, high ideals, philanthropy, luck, expansiveness, and ideas about social justice and civilization (ruled by Jupiter)

10th House: career, responsibility, honor and dishonor, perceptions of authority, relationships with authority figures, relationships with business and political power structures, responsibility, hard work, limitations, social standing, public reputation, and business (ruled by Saturn)

11th House: humanitarian endeavors, social ideals, group work, intellectual creative expression, desire to change social and political structures, contrariness, rebelliousness, invention and innovation, progressiveness, change, and personal freedom (ruled by Uranus)

12th House: the subconscious mind, self-sacrifice, intuition, miracles, secret knowledge, martyrdom, spiritual joy and sorrow, imagination, dreams, brilliance, madness, sensation-seeking, self-destruction, addiction, compassion, kindness, the ability to transcend boundaries, confusion, deception (of others and oneself), and altruism (ruled by Neptune)

Angular Planets

Angular planets are planets located along the axis – in other words, planets that fall along the line where the 12th house joins the 1st house, the 3rd house joins the 4th house, the 6th house joins the 7th house, and the 9th house joins the 10th house. Of these, the line that separates the 12th house from the 1st house and the line that separates the 9th house from the 10th house are considered the most important.

Planets that fall where the 12th house joins the 1st house will have a particularly strong effect on overall personality. Planets at this location are called rising planets, so a person with Uranus on the cusp of the 12th and 1st houses will be strong in the areas ruled over by Uranus and show traits of the sign that Uranus rules (Aquarius).

Planets located on the midheaven, which is the cusp of the 9th and 10th houses, also have a very strong effect on certain aspects of personality, particularly career aptitudes and choices. Rising and midheaven planets are some of the most important factors in a person's chart, though IC planets (those located on the cusp of the 3rd and 4th houses) and descending planets (located on the cusp of the 6th and 7th houses) can also have an effect.

The IC provides insights into the self that is seen by those closest to us, such as family, as well as our family structure.

The descendant, or cusp of the 6th and 7th houses, indicates the sorts of people we are attracted to. Theoretically, we should be most attracted to the sign of our descendant (directly opposite our ascendant).

Some astrologers believe that people who have many angular planets are more likely to become famous at some point during their lives.

Aspects

Aspects are the angles the planets formed in relation to one another at the time of a person's birth. The aspects considered most important include the conjunction, sextile, square, trine, inconjunct, and opposition.

Conjunction: A conjunction occurs when two planets are 0 degrees apart – in other words, right next to one another. This powerful aspect is often beneficial, though not always, because if the two planets involved are in negative aspect to many other planets, the conjunction can intensify the problems associated with the difficult aspects.

Planets in conjunction are working together, and their influence will have a major effect on personality. People with planets in conjunction often have one or two extremely well-developed talents or aptitudes, and many people who invent things or are responsible for medical breakthroughs have conjunctions or stelliums (more than two planets in conjunction). Having three or more planets in conjunction can indicate genius in a certain area.

Sextile: A sextile occurs when two planets are 60 degrees apart. Sextiles are beneficial aspects that create opportunities.

Unlike the trine, which simply drops good fortune in a person's lap, the sextile presents opportunities in the areas ruled by the planets involved in the sextile, and it is up to the individual to seize these opportunities and make something of them.

Square: A square occurs when two planets are 90 degrees apart. Squares are stressful or challenging aspects. Having squares in a natal chart often encourages creativity and ambition, as squares bring obstacles that must be overcome and strife that inspires the individual to develop necessary strengths and use creative problem solving abilities. Squares can promote character development because they ensure that life never becomes too easy.

Trine: Trines occur when two planets are 120 degrees apart. Trines are the most positive and harmonious aspects, bringing good fortune, ease, advantage, and luck in the areas ruled over by the planets involved in the trine.

Inconjunct (Quincunx): An inconjunct occurs when two planets are 150 degrees apart. The effects of the inconjunct are unpredictable, though often problematic.

An inconjunct can indicate stress, health problems, weaknesses, challenges, and obstacles in the personality or the environment that must be overcome. Some astrologers believe that the inconjunct (also known as a quincunx) brings the type of challenges that create wisdom.

Opposition: An opposition occurs when two planets are 180 degrees apart. Oppositions are difficult aspects that can bring discord, stress, chaos, and irritation, but like squares they tend to promote creativity, strength, and character development. It is more productive to view them as challenges rather than problems.

References

Bugler, C. (Ed.). (1992). *The Complete Handbook of Astrology*. Marshall Cavendish Ltd., Montreal.

Castille, D. (2000). *Sunny Day for a Wedding*. Les Cahiers du RAMS.

Fenton, S. (1989). *Rising Signs*. HarperCollins, London.

Heese, A. (2017). Cafe Astrology. CafeAstrology.com.

Quigley, J.M. (1975). *Astrology for Adults*. Warner Books, New York.

Rowe, P. *The Health Zodiac*. Ashgrove Press, Bath.

Sachs, G. (1998). *The Astrology File: Scientific Proof of the Link Between Star Signs and Human Behavior*. Orion Books, London.

Woolfolk, J.M. (2001). *The Only Astrology Book You'll Ever Need*. Madison Books, Lanham, MD.

Image Credits

All images were obtained from PublicDomainFiles.com:

- A pair of hearts: Mogwai
- Alianças (rings): Adassoft
- Basket with Apples: Larisa Koshkina
- Broken heart: Maqndon
- Business people silhouettes: Asrafil
- Dolphins: Dr. Mridula Srinivasan
- Egypt: US Air Force
- Faces: Inky2010
- Father walking with his children: CDC/Amanda Mills
- Girl on the beach practicing yoga: Anna Langova
- Hands with hearts: Petr Kratochvil
- Hearts: Vera Kratochvil
- Jigsaw: Yuri196
- Laptop computer: Metalmarious
- Love of books: George Hodan
- Money grabber: Johnny_automatic
- Night sky with moon and stars: George Hodan
- Penguins: Merlin 2525
- Scales of Justice: Laobc
- Silhouetted kiss: Dear_theophilus
- Stethoscope: Johnny_automatic
- Women playing soccer: US Air Force
- Young girl playing on the beach: CDC/Amanda Mills

Made in United States
North Haven, CT
04 November 2021